CARL WALKER:

THE SOUND OF JUSTICE

MAJESTE PHILLIP

All inquiries or sales request should be addressed to:

Planting People Growing Justice Press
P.O. Box 131894
Saint Paul, MN 55113
www.ppgjli.org

Printed and bound in the United States of America
First Edition
LCCN: 2024950487
1-9781959223603/9781959223597-11/15/24

DEDICATION

To my beloved community, may we never grow weary of
being instruments for the sound of justice, ringing loud and
strong for generations to come.

TABLE OF CONTENTS

Words in **bold** are in the glossary.

THE KID WITH THE BOX PIANO

Carl Walker has always loved music. As a child, he would put two boxes on top of each other and pretend they were a piano. He would imagine his audience cheering, "**Encore!** Encore! Well done!"

As Walker got older, he did not see a stage with only him on it. He saw a stage with hundreds of people who looked like him. All of them were talented and full of music.

Walker made it his life goal to use music to uplift his community. He became a well-known musician. He became a pastor. He even started a successful music school, Walker West Music Academy. Over the years, he has brought the joy of music to thousands of people of all ages.

CHAPTER 1:
THE CALL TO MUSIC

Carl Walker was born in East Saint Louis, Illinois, in 1939. He has a big family. His parents did not have much money, but they had faith and music. Walker often watched his father and grandmother play piano at the Church of God in Christ. His face would light up with joy. "I can't wait to play like that one day!" he'd say to himself.

His family eventually bought a piano. Walker knew they could not pay for him to take piano lessons, though. He started teaching himself. At church services, Walker would listen closely to the melodies he heard. Then he would go home and practice until his hands got tired.

One Sunday morning when Walker was around nine years old, the lead singer at church asked for someone to play for him while he sang. Walker was shy, but he knew this was his moment. He raised his hand and walked right up to the piano at the front of the church. He played beautifully.

The singer thought Walker was so talented that he offered to pay for piano lessons. Walker's teacher was Ms. Margarine Olive. She made Walker practice to perfection. She was tough on him because she believed in him. Walker decided that he would be a music teacher one day too.

FACT: TOUGH BEGINNINGS

Life was hard in 1939 when Walker was born.

The Great Depression had left many families without money.

World War II was about to begin.

For Black families, racism was an added struggle.

CHAPTER 2:
PATH TO PURPOSE

Carl Walker knew that going to school would help him reach his dreams. He graduated from Lincoln High School in 1956. But he did not stop there. A scholarship gave him the money he needed to go to McKendree College in Illinois. He majored in music.

After Walker graduated in 1960, he was invited to continue his music studies at MacPhail College in Minneapolis, Minnesota. This was one of the top music schools in the **Midwest**. He was proud to be one of the few African American students to receive this opportunity.

Walker's move to Minnesota led him to meet a beautiful and caring woman named Linda. He married her in 1968, and they raised five sons.

Together he and his wife taught their children to love God and music.

Walker gave many musical performances in Minnesota and Illinois. He also had a job that allowed him to support his family. He spent twenty years working for St. Joseph's Hospital in Saint Paul. He started as an admissions clerk. Eventually, he became head of the department. He was the first African American man to have this position.

One night in the late 1970s, Walker's life took a new turn. He felt the Lord tell him to become a preacher. He was nervous at first, but he found the courage to return to school. He attended North Central University in Minneapolis. Often, he was the only Black man in his classes. He had to work twice as hard to be seen as equal, but he did not let that stop him. He studied to become a pastor and started preaching in 1983.

In the late 1980s, Walker became a minister of music at Camphor Memorial United Methodist Church in Saint Paul. He prepared the choir to sing new hymns. He made sure the band sounded just right. Each Sunday, he used music to touch the souls of those around him.

Walker had already accomplished so much, but he wanted to do more to help others. All around him, he saw people without homes, struggling to pay bills. In 1992 at age 53, he started his own church in Saint Paul. Morning Star Missionary Baptist Church became known for its shelter program. Walker worked with a Catholic group to shelter up to forty people each night. Walker helped people in his community find housing—and hope and faith as well.

FACT

One of the African American musicians Carl Walker admired was Nat King Cole. Cole was a smooth **jazz** singer.

In 1956, Cole became the first African American performer to host a variety TV series.

CHAPTER 3:
LEAP OF FAITH

As Reverend Walker was starting his church, he was also working on other big plans. One of his good friends was a gifted Black musician named Grant West. They shared the same vision. They both felt that teaching music could help bring justice to the community.

Walker and West knew that, often, Black musicians were not given the same chances as other musicians. Some people even felt that music with Black roots was not worth hearing because it did not come from **Western** culture. The two friends believed a space was needed to celebrate African American music and **culture**. They hoped to create that space together.

In 1987, Carl Walker and Grant West started giving piano lessons in their homes. On Saturdays, all anyone could hear was the piano! One of Walker's students offered to let them give piano lessons in his apartment building, but that was not a long-term solution. It was time to find their own building.

On a cold winter night in 1988, they found a place they liked. It was in the Rondo neighborhood in Saint Paul. They moved in on New Year's Eve.

The building needed many repairs, so Walker and West leaned on the community for support. They gave piano lessons in exchange for helping to fix the building. All that hard work was worth it. Reverend Walker and Grant West officially opened Walker West Academy in 1992.

Together, Walker and West created a teaching style meant to give their students confidence. Students walk out of their very first lesson knowing how to play a simple melody. They learn to trust what they hear.

The music school started out small, but it grew every year. Today, students can learn to play a variety of instruments, such as violin, trumpet, saxophone, drums, and even organ. They can take voice lessons and sing in choruses. They can perform **classical music, jazz, hip-hop**, and more.

To make space for more students, the academy moved to a different building on Selby Avenue in 2014. Each week, Walker West serves several hundred students of all ages. It employs more than forty instructors. Many of the teachers are African American men who are often not represented in educational settings. This is another way that Walker West is special.

FACT: HYMNS THROUGH HISTORY

The Tuskegee Institute is a Black college in Alabama. It is home to the famous Tuskegee Institute Singers.

For more than a century, this singing group has honored the **spirituals** and hymns that were sung during slavery.

RECONNECT RONDO

Rondo is a large Black community in
St. Paul.

In the late 1950s, it was split in two
by the construction of Interstate 94.
Hundreds of people were forced out of
their homes. Many businesses closed
and never re-opened.

But the Rondo neighborhood never
lost its strong sense of identity.

CHAPTER 4:
LEGACY

For more than thirty years, Walker West Academy has given people the musical skills to tell their own stories. Many Walker West students have had great musical careers. Some have even played in the White House and on other national stages. Saint Paul mayors Chris Coleman and Melvin Carter were both students.

When Walker West opened, nearly all of the students were Black. Today, about half of the students are Black. Still, the offerings remain rooted in the African American experience. People of all backgrounds are invited to gather, explore, and grow through music.

Walker himself has taught music for more than fifty-five years.

"Music to me will always be a connector to people, no matter who they are," Walker says.

Now in his eighties, Reverend Carl Walker is still dreaming big. He imagines people from all over the world coming to Walker West. He wants them to experience true African American culture through music education.

His dream may just be within reach. Walker West Academy recently put together funding for another expansion. Soon the school will have a larger building, still in the Rondo community. There will be a recital hall, a recording studio, a technology lab, and outdoor spaces.

Reverend Carl Walker hopes to continue using music to heal the African American community. He is helping them remember the seeds of strength that were planted by their **ancestors**. He is helping people to add their own melodies to the sound of justice. This is the power of music.

ABOUT THE AUTHOR

Majeste Phillip is a passion-filled creative person, striving to utilize her gift of writing to challenge and inspire the world. She has contributed written work for two published books, *We Are the Dreams of Our Ancestors* and *Aya Anthology*.

From a young age, she has been fueled by the desire to help create a more just society. Majeste is currently pursuing her own pathway to law and justice. She is working for the State of Minnesota and plans to continue her education in law school. She enjoys learning about new art forms and gaining inspiration for her own creative work.

WAYS TO MAKE A DIFFERENCE

Don't be afraid to try something new. Reverend Walker made a difference because he wasn't afraid to do things he had never done before.

Look for ways to share kindness and teach others something you've learned. We all have gifts and talents that can be shared with others. We must be sure we are being kind as we help others learn something they may not know. Like Carl Walker and Grant West, we can help make a difference together.

Remember that "Practice Makes Permanent." One of Carl Walker's greatest qualities was his willingness to keep on practicing so he could perform at his very best. This took hours of going over the same music nonstop. But once he had the music locked in his mind, the possibilities were endless.

Don't be afraid to ask for help. Teamwork makes the dream work. Reverend Walker had a strong friendship with Grant West. The two friends shared the responsibility of running their music school. It is good to have someone we can lean on when we need some extra help in life.

Discover your roots. Reverend Walker knew his roots came from his history. He did not look at his upbringing with shame. Instead, he embraced it. His roots gave him purpose and a reason to work. hard. Knowing your roots means getting in touch with where you come from so you can be confident in where you are going.

GLOSSARY

Admissions	Officially allowing someone to enter an institution such as a hospital or school
Ancestors	Family members from long ago
Classical music	Serious music from the Western tradition
Culture	The traditions, arts, and achievements that develop over time in a particular place
Disc jockey	A person who selects and plays recorded music on the radio
Encore	Extending a performance due to the audience's enthusiasm
Great Depression	A time of extreme economic hardship during the 1930s
Hip-Hop	A type of music that was developed in the early 1970s by Black, Caribbean, and Latino youth in the Bronx in New York City

Jazz	American music known for its rhythms and accents. Jazz melodies may be made up by musicians as they play
Midwest	An area made up of twelve states in the north central part of the United States
Rhythm and Blues (R & B)	African American music with a strong beat. It was a forerunner to rock and roll
Soul music	A type of music rooted in African American culture. It often expresses deep feelings about love and hardship
Spirituals	Songs from the religious traditions of enslaved Black people in the southern United States
Swing Music	A style of jazz that has a flowing rhythm and is easy to dance to
Western	Relating to the traditions that developed over time in certain European countries.
World War II	A war involving many countries that took place between 1939 and 1945

BOOKS

Asim, Jabari. (2002). *A Child's Introduction to Jazz: The Musicians, Culture, and Roots of the World's Coolest Music (A Child's Introduction Series).* Black Dog & Leventhal.

Erskine, Kathryn. (2017). *Mama Africa! How Miriam Makeba Spread Hope with Her Song.* Farrar Straus Giroux.

Rockliff, Mara. (2018). *Born to Swing: Lil Hardin Armstrong's Life in Jazz.* Calkins Creek.

Weatherford, Carole Boston. (2008). *Before John was a Jazz Giant.* Henry Holt and Co.

WEBSITES

African American Music Facts for Kids:
https://kids.kiddle.co/African-American_music

Black History Songs for Kids Playlist:
https://www.youtube.com/
playlist?list=PLPN3oLV0UO5qhhP9-7KpbZiYjQPYmhmdU

Mr. Pete's Playhouse. I am the Dream|Black History Songs for Kids:
https://www.youtube.com/watch?v=fCXiqLgf-qk

Noodleloaf. Black History Month Songs for Kids:
https://www.noodleloaf.com/blog/black-history-month-songs-for-kids

SOURCES

Melo, Frederick, "Walker West Music Academy closing in on $12 million relocation, expansion in St. Paul," Saint Paul Pioneer Press, June 11, 2023.

Phillip, M. (2023, September 27). 9-27-23 Reverend Walker Interview. Other.

Walker, Mercedes, "Where it all started," April 18, 2021, Soul Lab Music LLC, https://www.soullabmusicllc.com/post/st-paul-living-legend.

WALKER | WEST. "About Us," 2024. https://walkerwest.org/about-us/.

ABOUT PLANTING PEOPLE GROWING JUSTICE LEADERSHIP INSTITUTE

Planting People Growing Justice Leadership Institute seeks to plant seeds of social change through education, training, and community outreach.

All proceeds from this book will support the educational programming of Planting People Growing Justice Leadership Institute.